Radiant Shadows

In the park, we chase our hats,
With squirrels that steal our snacks.
You trip on laces, I laugh loud,
Together, we're a goofy crowd.

Your dance moves, a sight to behold,
Like a jellyfish in waves, uncontrolled.
We juggle dreams, forget the rest,
In this odd mess, we're so blessed.

Eternal Bloom in the Garden of Us

We plant our doubts with seeds of cheer,
Water them daily, with laughter here.
Petals of puns, bloom with delight,
In the garden, we grow, oh so bright.

Bees think we're strange, buzzing around,
But we're just two clowns, joyfully bound.
Sunshine and giggles make weeds disappear,
In our patch of smiles, perfection draws near.

Interwoven Journeys

Two tangled ropes, we walk the line,
Tripping on life, but feeling fine.
Your wild ideas, my quirk in tow,
Crafting a tale, we laugh and grow.

Maps are for people who lose their way,
We wander aimlessly, day by day.
With snacks in pockets, and hearts in sync,
Every wrong turn makes us rethink.

Symphony of Two

Our laughter, a melody, bright and clear,
Offbeat notes when you dance near.
You sing off-key, but I don't mind,
In this duet, joy is defined.

The world is our stage, with curtains torn,
A harmony found in the day we were born.
With every mishap, the music plays sweet,
Together, my friend, we can't be beat.

Embracing the Infinite Tapestry

In a world of mismatched socks,
We dance like chickens, silly mocks.
A tapestry woven with quirks and laughs,
Our love's a puzzle with quirky halves.

We juggle life like oranges, too,
And sing off-key in our crazy zoo.
Every laugh is a stitch we weave,
In this crazy quilt, we believe.

Harmonies in Eternal Bloom

Like daisies in a field so bright,
We trip on roots, but hold on tight.
Our laughter echoes beneath the sun,
In blooms of joy, we always run.

You steal my fries and I steal a kiss,
In this mad dance, there's pure bliss.
Harmonies that make the neighbors stare,
Yet we just giggle without a care.

Love's Perpetual Symphony

With spoons as drums, we start to play,
In our kitchen band, come what may.
The spatula's a mic, the fridge a stage,
With every heartfelt note, we engage.

Our symphony's loud, it spills the beans,
We're serenading in mismatched jeans.
With every quirky dance and song,
It feels like this is where we belong.

Unfading Echoes of Affection

You tell the jokes and I laugh too loud,
In a crowd of two, we form our crowd.
With sticky notes and silly plans,
Love echoes on like clumsy hands.

In every glance, there's a wink that shines,
We make each other laugh with silly lines.
Unfading echoes of joy we share,
In our comedic tale, we dance with flair.

Heartstrings in Twilight

Balloons drift high, but so do pies,
We chase the clouds as the seagull flies.
With mismatched socks and silly hats,
We jam on spoons, like two cool cats.

The twilight glimmers with giggles bright,
We dance with shadows, what a sight!
Our laughter echoes in the fading day,
As twilight swirls our worries away.

Luminous Journeys Beyond Time

We zoom through dreams on rainbow tracks,
With silly songs and fuzzy snacks.
Each wobbly turn, a twist in fate,
Grinning wide, we just can't wait.

In this wild ride, the clocks all freeze,
Giggling past the space-time knees.
We high-five stars and toast with juice,
Time bends when laughter's on the loose.

Illuminated Footprints in Sand

Footprints sparkling, we run around,
With laughter glistening, what a sound!
Chasing waves that kiss our toes,
Building castles, making foes.

A seagull stole our snacks, oh no!
Chasing it down, we put on a show.
With sandy hair, we twirl and spin,
In this silly game, we always win.

Colliding Dreams in Space

In cosmic carts, we zoom and dart,
With comets waving, oh what art!
We launch our hopes to the moon's embrace,
Floating through time in a goofy race.

Stars shoot past like candy canes,
Each giggle echoes through the lanes.
As planets dance in a joyful swirl,
We twirl together, our laughter unfurl.

Fleeting Moments

In a feathered hat, we prance around,
Chasing shadows, giggles abound.
A dance with squirrels, we take the leap,
While ducks quack secrets, oh so deep.

With ice cream drips down our joyful chins,
We race the sun, where laughter begins.
A wink, a jest, in a puddle we splash,
Life's a bright blur, in a hilarious dash.

Lasting Love

You stole my fries, I stole your heart,
With every giggle, we play our part.
Two goofy souls entwined in a jest,
In the game of love, we're truly blessed.

From socks that don't match to silly faces,
Together we conquer the strangest places.
Your laugh is the song my heart sings loud,
In our soap bubble, we float like a cloud.

A Symphony Beyond Days

We dance with rainbows on our toes,
In a world where anything goes.
With kazoo concerts in the living room,
We summon joy like a flower in bloom.

Note by note, our laughter resounds,
A wacky tune that knows no bounds.
In the orchestra of our silly lives,
Our hearts strum melodies that forever thrive.

Embrace of the Infinite

Caught in a whirlwind of giggles and grins,
We spin like tops, when the fun begins.
Your hugs are like bubbles, so soft and sweet,
A carnival ride, my favorite treat.

With tacos for dinner and jelly for toast,
We toast to the chaos we love the most.
In an endless embrace where joy holds sway,
We're two quirky souls, come what may.

Tides of Our Togetherness

Riding waves of whimsy on boats made of twine,
We laugh at the silly, savor the brine.
With each ebb and flow, our humor grows high,
In a sea of laughter, we soar and we fly.

Time capes and jellybeans whirl in the air,
We toss them like dreams without a care.
On tides of togetherness, we paddle along,
In a melody of laughter, our hearts beat strong.

The Love We Paint

We splatter joy like Jackson Pollock,
With mismatched socks and silly talk.
Our hearts a canvas, bright and wild,
Each silly joke, a cherished child.

You draw the sun, I sketch the moon,
Together we create a goofy tune.
With paint-stained hands, we dance around,
In this wacky world, pure love is found.

Bound by the Infinite

Our love's a loop of endless yarn,
Twisted around, like a playful barn.
With each pull, a giggle breaks,
In our web of laughs, the world awakes.

Your smile's a comet, zipping by,
While I leap around, like a fly.
We're bound by laughter, in the sky's embrace,
Two silly beings, in our happy place.

Infinite Whispers of Togetherness

We speak in whispers, like playful ghosts,
Sharing secrets and mismatched toasts.
Each giggle's a promise, a shared delight,
In our silly realm, everything's right.

Your quirks are treasures, shining bright,
Like dancing stars on a moonlit night.
With whispers loud enough to break the norm,
Our love's a tempest, a laughing storm.

Timeless Reflections in Serenity

In a mirror of chuckles, we see our fate,
A wobbly dance that we celebrate.
With goofy grins, we light the way,
Turning dull moments into a grand ballet.

We reflect the joy of days gone by,
In silly selfies, we reach for the sky.
Timeless are the laughs that bind us tight,
In our cozy world, everything's bright.

Notes from the Heart's Symphony

In the orchestra of our days,
You play the kazoo in a million ways.
Your laughter sings, like a silly tune,
Dancing with stars, under the moon.

We waltz through puddles, splash and slide,
With goofy grins, there's no need to hide.
Our hearts compose a clumsy beat,
As we trip over shoelaces on this comedic street.

The coffee spills, but we just cheer,
Creating chaos, spreading love here.
A symphony of quirks, a joyful noise,
In a world that needs more silly joys.

So here's a toast to whimsy and cheer,
With you, my friend, I have no fear.
In laughter's embrace, let's always stay,
Creating a masterpiece, come what may.

Infinite Light of Connection

Your bright ideas are wildly surreal,
Like a cat in a hat, doing cartwheel.
We dance through mishaps, in the bright sun,
With jokes that land, like a bumbling run.

Like fireflies buzzing in a funny show,
Our hearts glow brightly, stealing the glow.
We mix up words, hilariously wrong,
But in our laughter, we always belong.

You say potato, I say tomatillo,
Creating a riddle, oh what a thrill-o!
Through ups and downs, we find our light,
Navigating darkness, with laughter so bright.

In this cosmic dance, we float and glide,
With puns and smiles, wrapped side by side.
An infinite glow, our spirits collide,
In this humorous connection, we take pride.

Wandering Through an Everlasting Dream

On fluffy clouds, we take our flight,
With socks on our hands, what a silly sight!
We tumble through rainbows, giggling wide,
In this dreamland, adventures reside.

With ice cream cones stuck to our nose,
We dance with the flowers, in silly throws.
Lost in a maze of whipped cream and cheer,
Every twist and turn, we hold dear.

A parade of ducks in bright, silly hats,
Chasing them down, amidst silly chats.
Through whimsical forests, we hop and skip,
With bursts of laughter, oh what a trip!

In this never-ending, giggly scheme,
Our hearts beat wildly, like a goofy dream.
So let's wander forever, hand in hand,
In this fairytale world, so funny and grand.

Woven Threads of Kindred Spirit

In the tapestry of life, we spin our thread,
With mismatched colors, never misled.
A patchwork of quirks, our stories entwine,
Each stitch a giggle, so bright and divine.

With buttons and sequins, we craft our fun,
Two silly souls, like two peas in one.
We knot our dreams in a colorful twist,
Creating a fabric that can't be missed.

Through the chaos of yarn, we find our way,
With laughter as glue, come what may.
We unravel together, no fear of the fray,
In this dance of friendship, we proudly sway.

So here's to the threads that bind us tight,
In this fabric of joy, everything feels right.
With love and laughter, let's weave our fate,
In this silly symphony, we'll celebrate!

Blossoming in Unison

In the garden, we both bloom,
Wearing hats made of cartoon.
Sunflowers giggle, daisies dance,
Caught in our continuous romance.

Bees buzz loud, we dance about,
Waving our arms, we twist, we shout.
Pollen on noses, what a sight,
Laughing together, hearts alight.

Roots entangled beneath the ground,
In our little world, joy is found.
Even weeds chuckle, join the show,
Together we sway, with nowhere to go.

Butterflies wink, as they flit near,
Whispering secrets only we hear.
In this garden, nothing can fuss,
All is well, just us being us.

Tapestries of Endless Views

Our laughter stitches every seam,
Patterns woven, a perfect dream.
Colors clash, yet they all blend,
In the fabric of love, we transcend.

A canvas splattered with silly hues,
Crayons marching, we can't lose.
In this patchwork, giggles reside,
Woven stories stitched side by side.

Exploring the hills, we roll down,
With each tumble, we lose a frown.
Painting skies with our silly schemes,
Chasing clouds, we craft our dreams.

Through every corner, a delightful find,
Treasures uncovered in heart and mind.
This tapestry holds the tales of us,
Crafted with joy, in laughter we trust.

Unfurling the Banner of Us

Flags waving high, we stand in place,
Banners of giggles, full of grace.
Colors bright, like our playful ways,
Making memories in sunny rays.

With each gust, the fabric flaps,
Echoes of laughter, joyful taps.
Your mismatched socks dance in the breeze,
A chaotic pattern, aiming to please.

Under the sun, we take a stand,
Waving hopes just like a band.
Every wave brings dreams anew,
Cheers of chaos, just me and you.

The world may scoff at our parade,
But in our hearts, joy is made.
With colors vibrant, a vision so grand,
Forever together, hand in hand.

Enchanted Landscapes of Affection

In this world, magic is found,
With trees that giggle, leaves that bounce around.
Mountains wear sweaters, cozy and warm,
In this landscape, love is the norm.

Rivers gurgle funny little rhymes,
Singing softly, skipping through time.
Every rock shares a silly secret,
Exploring here, we never regret.

The sun sprouts smiles, shining so bright,
Painting our days with pure delight.
Even the clouds wear jester hats,
Funny feelings shared with the cats.

In this enchanted world of ours,
Every moment, a sprinkling of stars.
With chuckles and joy, we venture and roam,
In this land of affection, we've built our home.

Boundless Glimmers of Connection

In a world of pizza pies,
We dance beneath the skies.
Your socks may not match,
But they sure bring a catch.

With laughter like a kite,
We take our silly flight.
Lost in a whirlwind of glee,
You and I, just carefree.

Each mishap, a spark,
Your quirks leave a mark.
Together we can run,
Chasing the setting sun.

Through puddles, we splash,
In this joy, we dash.
Hand in hand, no fuss,
Forever, just us.

Radiance in Unison

Our voices blend like jam,
A duet, that's who we am.
With you, I find my tune,
Bouncing to the light of the moon.

You wear that hat askew,
Like a superstar, it's true.
Dancing on our kitchen floor,
Who needs a dance club door?

Your laughter quakes the room,
Silly antics start to bloom.
Two goofballs in a whirl,
Pinching cheeks, give a twirl!

In our bubble, time stands still,
Like cotton candy, sweet thrill.
With every silly scheme,
Together, we live the dream.

Unwritten Chapters of Us

Each moment, a blank page,
In this whimsical stage.
With crayons, we scribble fate,
Making the mundane great.

From coffee spills to blunders,
We laugh through all the thunders.
These tales, they weave and bind,
A treasure trove we find.

You write the lines with flair,
Mismatched socks, no care.
Sipping tea, spilling beans,
In our wacky scenes.

There's magic in our jest,
In this oddball quest.
With every quirky tale,
Our bond will never fail.

Floating Through Infinite Skies

We drift on clouds of fluff,
Life's a rollercoaster, rough.
With rainbows wrapped in dreams,
Together, nothing seems.

Your jokes, they take me high,
Like balloons that touch the sky.
When hiccups come to play,
We giggle all the way.

In capes made of laughter,
We chase our happily ever after.
Through cosmic hugs, we soar,
No limits to explore.

In this vast, silly spree,
You and I, just meant to be.
With every silly twist,
This bond we can't resist.

Paths Intertwined in Perennial Joy

In a world where socks go missing,
We still find joy in the glistening.
Laughter echoes with each silly prank,
Together we float, our hearts like a tank.

Through puddles we splash with pure delight,
Chasing each other from morning till night.
You steal my fries, I steal your hat,
In this circus of love, we're both quite the brat.

With mismatched shoes and ice cream mustaches,
We conquer the world with our goofy clashes.
Sometimes we dance in grocery store aisles,
Creating a scene that ignites all the smiles.

So here's to us, in our comedic spree,
Two jesters in life's endless marquee.
Together we stumble, we twirl and we sway,
In this crazy duet, let's always replay.

Hues of Togetherness in Twilight

Under the stars, we paint with mischief,
Your brush is a banana, what a swift gift!
We giggle at clouds that resemble our dreams,
As we plot our adventures in moonlight beams.

A swinging balloon, you've let it fly high,
Chasing after it, both you and I.
We butt heads like goats in a friendly tease,
Finding our rhythm with the buzz of the bees.

Silly serenades in the cool evening breeze,
Our laughter ignites as the night starts to freeze.
With your funny faces and my silly puns,
We wander through twilight, oh what funny runs!

We wrap ourselves in stories and laughs,
Drawing our joy from the quirkiest halves.
In this twilight glow, we're whimsically free,
Creating new hues of togetherness, you see.

Beyond the Horizon of Us

Oh, the horizon, it bends with our cheer,
We race down the edge, daring the fear.
With flip-flops on, we trip on each bend,
Every giggle a treasure, every laugh a friend.

Seagulls squawk as we mimic their calls,
Building sandcastles where laughter befalls.
Our beach ball's a monster, but we take it in stride,
Tossing our worries far back with the tide.

Beyond the waves, our dreams take flight,
Two silly sailors casting hearts into night.
In this ocean of humor, we weave and we sway,
Navigating love in our comedic ballet.

So let's grab our maps, let's set off anew,
Adventurous capers are waiting for two.
With each goofy twist, we'll sail far and wide,
Beyond every horizon, with laughter as our guide.

Fireside Tales of Our Forever

Gather around for the tales of our days,
Where marshmallows melt in the silliest ways.
You tell of a bear that danced with a fox,
As I laugh so hard, I lose both my socks.

The fire crackles, our stories take flight,
You jump up and down, what a comical sight!
With shadows like monsters that dance on the wall,
We conquer our fears with each giggly call.

Remember the time we mistook logs for gold?
The treasure we sought, but our hearts just felt bold.
Every spark lights a memory filled with fun,
Toasting our marshmallows under the sun.

So let's weave our tales by the warm fireside,
With laughter as fuel, let our memories glide.
In this cozy moment, let our stories flow,
Forever entwined, in the warmth of our glow.

Melodies of Our Forever

We hum our tunes in silly ways,
Like cats who think they're pianos,
Singing off-key, yet full of cheer,
In this odd ballad of our years.

With sock puppets and wild dance moves,
We sway like leaves in gentle breeze,
Our laughter bounces off the walls,
A symphony of joyful tease.

From morning toast to midnight snacks,
We craft our songs of pure delight,
In university of life we learn,
That laughter is our best spotlight.

Together we spin a goofy world,
In hats that tilt and shoes that squeak,
Each echo of our quirky harmony,
A melody that makes us unique.

Dancing Amongst Stars of Memory

Two clumsy stargazers in a whirl,
Twinkle toes on cosmic floors,
We trip on dreams and stumble bright,
In this galaxy of warm rapport.

With every wish, our toes collide,
As we blame gravity for our landslide,
The planets laugh, the comets cheer,
In a dance that always feels so dear.

A two-step waltz on clouds of fluff,
Twists and turns, though never quite tough,
Bouncing off worlds, our giggles spread,
We're champions in this starry bed.

Juggling memories like juggling stars,
We toss and fumble, we laugh some more,
In this kaleidoscope of silly blinks,
Our hearts keep spinning, forever soar.

The Eternal Canvas of Companionship

Painting our lives in splashy hues,
With brushes made of giggles bright,
Each stroke a memory, dripping fun,
Our masterpiece shines in pure twilight.

With every blunder on the page,
We sprinkle in our quirkiest flair,
Coloring outside the perfect lines,
Creating chaos, love in the air.

In splatters of paint, we find our way,
Our laughter echoes like joyous art,
Every canvas tells a vibrant tale,
A testament to our joyful heart.

As portraits grow and twist anew,
Each misstep a brush of fate,
We'll frame our moments, one by one,
In a gallery that never waits.

Threads of a Never-Ending Story

We weave our tale in silly threads,
With looms of laughter, bright and bold,
Every stitch a giggle, each twirl a twist,
In this fabric of life, we unfold.

With spools of fumbles and patterns rare,
We craft adventures, loop by loop,
From tangled yarn to knots of cheer,
Our stories knit a joyful group.

As tales get taller, so do our dreams,
Spinning yarns of light and play,
In a tapestry spun from happy seams,
We celebrate our funny ballet.

Together crafting our endless yarn,
Winding our joys into playful sway,
Forever spinning our vibrant lore,
In a tale that won't ever fray.

Waves of Elysian Whispers

In the ocean of laughter we float,
Our goofy antics keep us remote.
Seagulls squawk as we splash like fools,
Riding waves, breaking all the rules.

Sandy toes and sunburnt noses,
Tickled by the wind, life composes.
With every tumble, every spin,
Our joy bursts forth, like waves within.

Chasing crabs, they scuttle away,
We trip on beach balls, they laugh and play.
Coconut drinks with tiny umbrellas,
Mixing sweet tales with silly propellers.

Sunset giggles paint the sky,
As day whispers secrets, we sigh.
In this paradise, carefree and free,
Life is a splash, just you and me.

Our Radiant Footprints in Time

Every step we take leaves a mark,
Dancing in chaos, igniting a spark.
With mismatched socks and silly hats,
We waddle down paths like happy cats.

Footprints fading in the sand,
Like clumsy ballet, we take a stand.
Make-over your shoes, here comes the clown,
Trip over giggles wearing a crown.

Side by side, in life's peculiar race,
We trip, we skip, with stylish grace.
Pulling faces, we conquer the grime,
Carving each moment, one silly rhyme.

In the tapestry of laughter we weave,
Giggles paint moments, oh my, believe.
Dancing shadows skip through our dreams,
Echoes of humor burst at the seams.

Everlasting Echoes of You and I

In the hall of mirrors, we make silly sounds,
Reflections laugh back, twisting around.
Your grin echoes as I stumble near,
Life's merry pranksters, spreading the cheer.

Every silly joke, every shared glance,
Fills the air like a ridiculous dance.
Time spins wildly, ticking like mad,
In this whirlwind, we're never sad.

Stumbling over stories with glee,
Our laughter rises like a playful spree.
In the chorus of life, we sing loud,
Creating a symphony, oh so proud.

Memories linger, as bright as a spark,
Leaving imprints, each silly remark.
In the echoes of joy, we'll find our way,
Forever as jesters, come what may.

The Infinity Within Our Hearts

In this circus of life, we juggle the fun,
Clowns at heart, beneath the sun.
With every balloon, we float and soar,
Creating a ruckus, asking for more.

Giggles and surprises create our art,
A canvas of chaos, straight from the heart.
With confetti storms and silly tricks,
We dance through life, with winks and clicks.

In the kaleidoscope of silly delight,
Every prank pulls us, holding us tight.
Time spins like a top, never to cease,
In this carnival joy, we find our peace.

With every heartbeat, our colors collide,
Painting the world with laughter as guide.
In this infinite jest, love's spark remains,
Eternally playful, like joy in our veins.

Canvas of Our Souls

In a world where socks don't match,
We dance like clumsy penguins, no catch.
With splattered paint on our shoes,
We create a masterpiece, no muse.

Laughing at our tangled hair,
We spin like tops without a care.
With every slip and every fall,
We embrace chaos, having a ball.

Our hearts are brushstrokes on the floor,
Painting love with laughter, we soar.
Each quirk and giggle makes us whole,
A canvas bright, our joyful soul.

Through silly moments and blushing fame,
We scribble life, no need for shame.
In this mess, we find our grace,
A colorful art, our funny space.

Luminous Threads of Connection

Tangled cords of life we weave,
A tapestry that we believe.
In jumbled texts and memes so bright,
We find our giggles in the night.

With puns and jokes, our hearts ignite,
Two goofy souls, what a sight!
Through wifi waves and phone calls late,
We share the laughs, we celebrate.

In sparkly sweaters and mismatched socks,
We dance through life like bumbling clocks.
Tied together, we spin and sway,
Connecting giggles in our play.

In every shared, ridiculous thought,
The warmth of joy that we've sought.
With luminous threads that tie us tight,
Our silly love shines through the night.

Ethereal Embrace

In a hug that's slightly askew,
We twirl like clouds in skies so blue.
With smiles that stretch from ear to ear,
Our goofy love makes it all clear.

Like marshmallows in a stormy tea,
We laugh, we spill, we're wild and free.
Floating high on a cotton candy cloud,
In every giggle, we're laughter proud.

As our goofy dance makes heads turn,
We share delight, igniting the burn.
With every jest and silly tease,
We float through life with perfect ease.

In this embrace that feels like flight,
Our laughter echoes through the night.
So here we are, two stars that shine,
In this funny waltz, forever divine.

The Art of Us

We paint the town in splashes bright,
With every joke, we take our flight.
Mistakes are merely brushstrokes bold,
Creating stories that never grow old.

With every quirk and silly face,
We craft a world, a funny space.
Like doughnuts tossed into the air,
We chase the joy, without a care.

In mismatched outfits, we strut around,
Our laughter blossoms, it's truly profound.
From breakfast spills to blundered words,
We sketch a life where joy's not blurred.

So here's to us, in goofy glee,
The art of love, wild and free.
Together, we create with zest,
A masterpiece that's simply the best.

Eternal Echoes of Us

In a world of mismatched socks,
We wander like confused clocks.
With cupcakes flying through the air,
Laughter's anthem, beyond compare.

Our silly games, a grand parade,
Like shadows on a moonlit glade.
Chasing squirrels while wearing a hat,
Making memories on a silly mat.

Every glance, a giggling quake,
We trip on words for fun's own sake.
In a dance of pure delight,
We spin and fall, oh what a sight!

With jellybeans in wishing wells,
We whisper loud, like secret spells.
In this maze where laughter flows,
Our friendship blooms, and joy just grows.

Whispers in the Twilight

In twilight's glow, we play charades,
Making shadows and silly trades.
With rubber ducks and wooden spoons,
We dance beneath the laughing moons.

Our stories blend like paint on walls,
A gallery of giggles and brawls.
Each whispered joke, a playful tease,
We bubble over like fizzy cheese.

The stars blink back as we conspire,
To ride the waves of our desire.
With silly hats and wiggling toes,
We frolic where the river flows.

Laughter echoes in the breeze,
Tickling softly like buzzing bees.
In a world where chaos reigns,
Our joyous bond forever gains.

Timeless Serenade

We sing a tune that's off the beat,
With off-key notes, we dance our feet.
Each awkward step, a cherished art,
Creating chaos from the heart.

Like raindrops falling on a train,
We mix our laughter with the rain.
In harmony of clumsy grace,
We waltz like snails in a silly race.

Our serenade, a hearty cheer,
With banana peels that draw us near.
In endless loops of joyful jest,
We find the fun that feels the best.

Through timeless nights, our spirits glow,
With hidden gems in every show.
In such a world of joyful fuss,
There's magic found in delightful us.

Celestial Dance of Hearts

In cosmic dreams, we twirl and sway,
With stars as partners in our play.
Like comets racing in a line,
We glow and giggle, oh so fine.

Our antics filled with cosmic spunk,
In space-time curls, we roll and clunk.
With alien hats and sparkly shoes,
We dance with joy while singing blues.

Each moonlit leap, a burst of fun,
Chasing sunsets 'til we're done.
In this universe of dreams,
Laughter ripples with radiant beams.

Though planets spin and time may part,
We share a dance that warms the heart.
In endless tales of joy and trust,
We shine as one, oh glorious us.

Fragments of Forever

In the garden of mismatched socks,
We dance like two bewildered clocks.
Your laugh a bubble, my grin a kite,
Together we chase the fading light.

Spilled coffee on the morning news,
Who knew that was our secret muse?
We tumble through the days with grace,
Like jellybeans in an empty space.

Unfading Radiance

Your hair a nest of morning toast,
I claim I'm the one who's the most.
We giggle at the soap that slipped,
In our house, the mess is well-equipped.

You wore my jacket, oh what a thrill,
As we walk up the hill with a giddy spill.
The sun plays tricks, it bends and sways,
Like shadows dancing in the haze.

Boundless Horizons Together

With pizza boxes as our throne,
We rule a kingdom made of foam.
Your jokes are cheese, mine are the bread,
Together we feast, no thought to dread.

We paint the sky with laughter's hue,
Whimsical clouds, just me and you.
As stars wink out like playful lights,
We scribble dreams on dusty nights.

Fleeting Moments

A hiccup here, a snort right there,
Our bloopers fill the evening air.
With mismatched shoes and quirky hats,
We dance through life like silly bats.

The fridge is bare, we munch on toast,
But in our hearts, we need it most.
We build a castle with old newspapers,
Fortress of laughter and funny capes.

Lasting Light

When you trip over the garden gnome,
I laugh, it feels like home.
We tidy up with playful jests,
Our love a game, we'll never rest.

The world spins like a teacup ride,
You hold on tight; I'm by your side.
In every quirk and silly scene,
We find the magic in the routine.

Mystical Moments Under the Moon

Under the moon, we twirl and spin,
Chasing shadows, wearing grins.
Laughter echoes in the night,
While stars giggle, oh what a sight!

You trip over your own two feet,
I snort at you, it's quite the feat.
Moonlight bounces off your nose,
Secretly wishing you'd strike a pose!

We pretend to be wise and old,
While whispering tales that never get told.
With each wink, shadows play hide and seek,
Our hearts giggle, feeling so chic!

So here we dance, forever free,
A comedy show, just you and me.
With cosmic giggles and silly grins,
These mystical moments never wear thin.

While Time Stands Still for Us

In a world where clocks take a snooze,
We choose to wear our wackiest shoes.
Tick-tock? No way, we just ignore,
As we launch into laughter, who needs more?

Past the hours and the tock of the clock,
You juggle dreams while I dance on a rock.
Time's a joker, just laugh it away,
Together we'll seize this silly ballet!

Napping on clouds, oh what a sight,
In pajamas made of pure moonlight.
The day can't find us, lost in our fun,
While giggles rise as bright as the sun!

With every moment stretching like taffy,
You're the sweet sprinkle, making me happy.
Together we create a timeless fuss,
This here is just for the both of us!

Unending Skies of Affection

With a sky so vast, we get lost in bliss,
As we share our dreams with a cosmic kiss.
Clouds shaped like puppies, we watch and stare,
Laughing so hard, we float in midair!

You claim the stars are just giant bugs,
I'm holding your hand and giving you hugs.
Together we ponder the silliest things,
In this universe, joy is what sings!

Rocketing laughter to galaxies wide,
We're each other's funny, galactic guide.
No far-off planet can ever compare,
To this endless sky and the love that we share!

Through the stars, as we tumble and dive,
You squeeze my heart; oh, we're so alive!
With our cosmic banter, we'll float and roam,
In this unending sky, we've built our home.

Dance of Shadows and Light

In the flicks of shadows, we sway and glide,
Our laughs echo, oh what a ride!
Each flicker of light spins tales untold,
As we dance through with hearts made of gold.

Around the fire, we jump and cheer,
Your goofy faces always bring me near.
Shadows become our magical friends,
In this witty world, the fun never ends!

Flickering lanterns brighten the night,
While shadows pull pranks that give us a fright.
You step on my toes, we both erupt,
In this playful magic, we're joyfully stuck!

As darkness battles with sparks of the dawn,
You laugh so hard, you could sprout a fawn.
With every twirl in this dazzling flight,
We're dancing our dream, our spark, our light!

Fragments of Forever

In a world of mismatched socks,
We dance through life in silly clogs.
You steal my fries, I sip your drink,
Yet in this chaos, we always sync.

Your hair's a mess, my shirt's too bright,
We laugh until it's late at night.
Two peas in a pod, or maybe five,
In this quirky spree, we feel alive.

We argue on which movie to see,
But popcorn fights are the remedy.
With every laugh, the moments grow,
Our happy mess is the best show.

Through silly pranks and pillow fights,
You're my delight, my favorite sights.
Together, we're a joyful spree,
In our mad world, just you and me.

Serenading Dreams of Togetherness

Dreams of tacos and late-night fries,
Okay, let's be honest, it's a surprise.
We chase down stars on a lopsided bike,
As if this path was something we'd like.

You sing off-key, while I crack a grin,
This duet makes the life we're in.
We hiccup through jokes, we tumble and fall,
Our laughter, a melody, binding us all.

Your antics are bright, my puns are absurd,
Like two little birds, chirping unheard.
We twirl through the night, with dreams that amuse,
In the wackiest tales, we never lose.

With pranks and schemes, we venture and roam,
In this wild world, we've carved a home.
Hand in hand, with a wink and a nudge,
In this life of chaos, we'll never judge.

Celestial Waters of Shared Souls

Splashing in puddles, a whimsical glee,
As fish in a pond, we swim wild and free.
With stars in our eyes, and mud on our shoes,
Together we jest, with nothing to lose.

We dive into dreams, like ducks in a stream,
Your laughter's infectious, it fuels my beam.
As jellybeans dance in a rainbow swirl,
You make me feel like a dizzying whirl.

With towels as capes, we conquer the day,
In our little kingdom, we always play.
Sipping on lemonade under the sun,
Sharing our secrets, each laugh, oh what fun!

From clouds or from fishbowl, the view's always bright,
With goofy grins, we chase the twilight.
Floating through life, in this giggly sea,
What a joy it is, just you and me.

The Unfolding Petals of Us

We bloom each morning, like flowers in spring,
With pollen-covered hearts, it's joy we bring.
You spill my coffee, I trip on a shoe,
Our clumsy dance is a sight to view.

Petals of laughter fly high in the air,
As snorts and giggles strip worries bare.
With every blunder, we find our way,
In a garden of joy, we choose to stay.

Your quirky socks, mismatched with flair,
We twirl through life without a care.
Amidst all the antics, love blooms, so bold,
In this wild fearless garden, we let joy unfold.

With sunshine warmth, through storms we roam,
In each other's quirks, we've found our home.
As petals scatter in a silly rush,
With hearts ever light, we bloom in a hush.

Never-Ending Horizons of Us

In a world where socks go missing,
We dance with mismatched socks, glistening.
Chasing sunsets with our laughter loud,
Two clowns in love, we stand so proud.

We play tag with the wind, oh what a sight,
Stumbling over dreams, giving pure delight.
Our road trips end up at the fridge,
As we feast on snacks, it's our own smidge.

With maps upside down, we wander on,
Every wrong turn feels like a song.
In our laughter, we find the way,
Through silly moments, we choose to stay.

Arm in arm, we stroll through the gray,
The skies hear our jokes, never dismay.
With hearts so full, we're always blessed,
The horizon's wide, but we're not stressed.

Orchard of Timeless Affection

In our garden, fruits hang low,
We giggle as the bunnies steal our show.
Each cherry red, a joke we share,
Nature's laughter echoes everywhere.

We prance through aisles of silly vines,
Where tomatoes sneak and prove their lines.
Every peach declares a little pun,
In this orchard, we bask in the sun.

With juice-smeared cheeks, we run and shout,
Growing our love with every doubt.
Each bite a treasure, sweet and bright,
In this charming chaos, everything's right.

Harvesting moments, our joy is wild,
In this whimsical world, we're nature's child.
With every giggle, our roots entwine,
In this orchard, our hearts align.

Celestial Dance of Soulmates

Stars waltz around, a cosmic jest,
We trip on galaxies, feeling blessed.
Our laughter echoes in the night sky,
As comets tease us with a wink, oh my!

We twirl like planets in the great expanse,
Each awkward move turns into a dance.
Galactic giggles fill the infinite air,
In this weird ballet, we throw up our hair.

With shooting stars, we toss our dreams,
Bouncing through stardust, nothing's as it seems.
In nebulae, our silly jokes reside,
In this universe, it's just you and I stride.

Hold my hand, let's fly so high,
As we count the planets and wave goodbye.
In this dance, we both play the fool,
Together we shine, in love's golden pool.

Threads Woven by Moonlight

Under the moon, the threads entwine,
With silly stories, our laughter shines.
We stitch together memories so bright,
In our quirky quilt, everything feels right.

Yarn balls roll like our silly chats,
Where every stitch is a dance, imagine that!
Tangled up in fabric, we're side by side,
In this cozy chaos, we choose to abide.

With needles clicking like a rhythmic song,
We patch our hearts, this is where we belong.
In every loop, our love is sewn,
Among the stitches, our secrets are grown.

By moonlight, we craft with glee,
Our tangled tales, wild as the sea.
In this tapestry of laughter and play,
Love's subtle thread lights up our way.

Skybound Lullabies of Togetherness

Floating high, we chase the clouds,
Giggles echo, laughter loud.
A pie in the sky, a burst of cheer,
With you, every moment is a souvenir.

Wobbly flights and silly falls,
We dance through the air, defying calls.
A nest made of wishes, dreams in tow,
In our goofy orbit, love starts to glow.

Tickled by the wind, we soar so free,
Your silly faces are a sight to see.
With wings made of joy and hearts unconfined,
In our laughter bubble, the world's redefined.

Together we drift on this giggly plane,
Your quirks, my spark, we'll never be mundane.
In the sky, where the fun gets serious,
Every jest we share feels mysteriously curious.

In the Garden of Infinite Moments

In a garden where the giggles grow,
We plant our dreams in a row.
With daisies that dance and tulips that sing,
We chase butterflies, love's sweet offering.

Your jokes are the weeds that tickle my heart,
In this floral playground, we never part.
Every petal whispers, 'Stay a while,'
Among the sunflowers, we share a smile.

The tomatoes blush, the peppers prance,
In our quirky garden, there's always a chance.
With dirt on our knees and grins without end,
Every moment here feels like a trend.

So let's gather the blooms of each silly day,
With rainstorms of laughter, come what may.
In this patch of wonder, just us two,
Every bruise from the giggles makes us anew.

Starlit Paths of Unity

Under the stars, we trip and stumble,
The cosmos giggles, our hearts still humble.
With moonlight paths that sparkle and twist,
In cosmic chaos, how could we resist?

Your one-liners shine brighter than stars,
In the great expanse, we balance on Mars.
With every wobbly step, we giggle and glide,
Together in orbit, we can't help but bide.

The Milky Way whispers, 'What a bizarre dance,'
Our laughter rockets, we take every chance.
In this universe where we're just a spark,
Our joy lights the way in the deep and dark.

So let's twinkle through space, hand in hand,
In our starry journey, so wonderfully planned.
With each pulse of humor, our bond grows bold,
For together, we shine in galaxies untold.

Unraveling the Infinite Embrace

In a hug that stretches across the skies,
We twist and tumble, oh what a surprise!
With arms like rubber bands, we bounce around,
In love's playful grip, our bliss is profound.

The more we squeeze, the more we unravel,
In this wacky ride, we learn to travel.
Your laughter is magic, my silly song,
In our wondrous embrace, where we both belong.

Every tickle turns into a raucous cheer,
With every goofy moment, we draw near.
With strands of delight, our hearts intertwine,
In this comical knot, we're doing just fine.

So here in our hug, let's spiral and spin,
With our giggly tapestry, we always win.
Filled with jests that cause delight,
We play in the arms of love each night.

Chasing the Horizon Hand in Hand

We run like kids with ice cream cones,
Our hearts in sync, with sugar tones.
The sun sets low, a golden race,
Trip on my shoelace, what a disgrace!

The wind whispers secrets, we giggle loud,
Pretending to be part of the crowd.
With goofy grins, we leap and pose,
As the sunset blushes, we strike a pose!

With every stride, we dance and dart,
Chasing shadows, a wild art.
Our laughter echoes, a silly tune,
Hand in hand, we'll bounce to the moon!

As night drapes stars on our heads,
We plot more pranks on sleepy beds.
With dreams to share, we scheme away,
The horizon calls; let's not delay!

Whirling Leaves of Change

The leaves are waltzing, swirling around,
In the crisp air, we're laughter bound.
I toss a leaf, it hits your nose,
You spin and swirl, my funny rose!

Autumn's here with its pumpkin spice,
Dancing with joy, we roll the dice.
Each leaf that falls is a giggle shared,
In nature's cradle, we're unprepared.

With scarves that tangle, and hats that fly,
You trip on a branch, and I can't lie—
A splendid sight, you tumble down,
Like a silly, soft, dramatic clown!

So let's catch the breeze, twirl side to side,
Through whirling leaves, our spirits glide.
The world's a stage, a playful chance,
In this autumn dance, let's take a chance!

Rivers of Us

We float like ducks down the wavy streams,
With rubber boots and silly dreams.
Splashing water, laughter bursts,
You mock a splash; oh, you're the worst!

With every ripple, our joys entwine,
Like curious fish, we sip on brine.
You catch a twig, I grab a leaf,
Our river's journey is beyond belief!

Bobbing along in the sunshine bright,
You attempt to fish, but it's quite a sight.
The fish play tag, they swim away,
While we end up rolling, in giggles we lay!

So let's ride the tides, just you and me,
In rivers of laughter, wild and free.
Our hearts hold stories, forever to keep,
Into the sunset, this treasure we reap!

Notes of a Timeless Song

We play the tune of a goofy song,
With off-key notes that seem all wrong.
Your voice is like a foghorn loud,
But it makes me smile, I'm so proud!

As we strum our way on the silly path,
Laughter aligns with a bubbling bath.
You dance like jelly in a fishy tank,
With crazy moves, oh what a prank!

With every beat, our spirits soar,
Creating melodies we can explore.
The world's our stage, the audience bliss,
In a duet of giggles, we can't miss!

So let's keep singing, no need for fame,
In this timeless dance, we'll play the game.
Our hearts compose a tune so sweet,
With funny laughter, we're never beat!

Whispers Carried by the Wind

In the park we laugh and dance,
Chasing dreams like kids at play.
Silly hats upon our heads,
Strangers stop to joke and sway.

Kites fly high, our secrets shared,
Windy tales of silly schemes.
Grass stains on our silly pants,
Oh, how we giggle at our dreams.

A squirrel stole your sandwich, friend,
We chase it down in pure delight.
Through the trees, we run and shout,
Life's small joys make every night.

So here we are, two clowns in sync,
With mismatched shoes and funny ties.
Painting joy with every blink,
In this comedic paradise.

When Stars Align in Harmony

Two stars twirling in the night,
Bouncing off the Milky Way.
Twirling snacks and sips of juice,
Making wishes come what may.

We sit beneath the twinkling lights,
Trading stories, laughter, cheer.
"Did you see that? Shooting star!"
I laughed, "Your hair is like a sphere!"

The cosmos laughs with us tonight,
In cosmic jokes we find our grace.
Alien ships doing the dance,
Celebrating our silly chase.

A melody of quirky dreams,
In harmony, we strut and swerve.
Together, making silly schemes,
As planets spin and laugh and curve.

Reflections of Our Timeless Bond

In every mirror, I see us clear,
Two troublemakers, bold and free.
Spitting jokes like water balloons,
Splashing laughter, you and me.

With silly faces in the glass,
Creating fun with every pose.
Close your eyes, just feel the glow,
Time races by, but never slows.

We stumble into shops and laugh,
Trying on the craziest hats.
Fashion queens of our own realm,
With furry boots and polka-dots.

Reflective laughs that never fade,
Every glance a burst of cheer.
In the glass, the joy cascades,
As our silly thoughts draw near.

The Canvas of Us Unveiled

Painting life with colors bright,
Splatters of joy, a funny refrain.
Dipping brushes in our dreams,
Each stroke tells our silly pains.

Trees of laughter, skies of smiles,
Our canvas chuckles with delight.
Every hue a memory made,
In our world, we paint the night.

A splash of blue for every joke,
A swirl of pink for silly dances.
With every giggle, laughter stoked,
Creating wild, whimsical prances.

The masterpiece is all around,
In every corner, laughter calls.
With funny tales and playful frowns,
Our canvas of joy forever sprawls.

Vows Etched in Eternity

In the garden where we roam,
We plant our dreams, call it home.
You trip on roots, I laugh out loud,
Two clowns in love, oh so proud.

When cookies burn and smoke alarms sing,
We dance in chaos, you twirl, I fling.
You steal my fries, I roll my eyes,
Yet in this madness, joy never dies.

The cat we named after a prince,
Steals our blankets, but we don't flinch.
His reign is grand, his style divine,
Ruling our hearts, a furry goldmine.

In silly fights, we toss some pillows,
Critics would say we're just two weirdos.
But in our laughter, the world fades wide,
Together, we're the best comic ride.

Seasons of Evermore

In winter's chill, we wear our scarves,
A fashion show, oh how we starve!
You strut like a model, I trip in glee,
Winter wonderland, just you and me.

When spring arrives, with blooms so bright,
You sneak up with mud—oh, what a sight!
From flower to flower, we play tag,
Covered in dirt, what a crazy brag!

Summer sun shines, we hit the beach,
You build a castle that's far from reach.
But waves crash down, a watery fight,
In the sandy chaos, we're pure delight.

Autumn leaves whisper, it's time to fly,
You catch a leaf, pretend to cry.
With laughter and snacks, we watch them fall,
In this funny dance, we have it all.

Portraits of an Infinite Heart

In magic pens, our stories ignite,
Crazy doodles fill every night.
I draw a monster, you sketch a cat,
Our love's a canvas—where's the spat?

Each morning greets with silly faces,
You wear my socks—what a mix of graces!
Coffee spills, and we giggle so loud,
A masterpiece made in our little crowd.

Your jokes are bad, but cheers, they bring,
A laughter symphony, we both can sing.
In every sketch, our quirks collide,
Together, we paint the world wide.

With crayons bright, we color outside,
In every line, our dreams abide.
A portrait of joy, forever and free,
Art from the heart, just you and me!

Cosmic Conversations of Us

Under the stars, we chat away,
You make up aliens, I laugh and sway.
Testing gravity with each silly thought,
A spaceship of dreams, oh what a plot!

The moon is jealous, we're shining bright,
You claim you're an astronaut, what a sight!
In every giggle, the cosmos gleams,
Together we build our wildest dreams.

Black holes lurking, we dodge and spin,
In the universe, let the fun begin!
With stardust sprinkled on every tale,
Our cosmic jokes are destined to sail.

From galaxies far to the Milky Way,
We toast to love, come what may.
In every laugh, the stars conspire,
Igniting our hearts with celestial fire.

Dreamcatchers in the Night

In the dark, we spin our dreams,
Catching giggles, oh how it seems!
Laughter echoes, sweet and bright,
Who knew sleep could feel so light?

Juggling pillows like a pro,
Sneaky snacks, oh look at us go!
A dance party with sleepy eyes,
Moonlight winks, and the pillow sighs.

We craft wishes from silly fears,
Whisper secrets, sip our cheers.
Starlit chases, fun just begun,
Joy spills over like a bubble gun!

So here we are, a whimsical pair,
In a dreamscape, floating in air.
With chuckles blooming in every corner,
We are the night's delightful performer!

The Light We Share

Two glowbugs in the evening glow,
Making silly shapes, just so you know.
Flickering laughter, bright and warm,
Explosive giggles, a shining swarm!

Crickets harmonize with our tune,
While shadows chuckle beneath the moon.
We chase the sparkles, dash and dive,
Who knew fun could feel so alive?

A lantern flicks, and we trade a grin,
In this wild glow, let the fun begin!
We're silly fireflies, buzzing in light,
Dazzling the world, from day to night.

So hold my hand, let's light the way,
In this adventure, let's laugh and play.
With every giggle, the shadows flee,
Together we shine, just you and me!

A Tapestry of Reflections

In the mirror, we're quite the sight,
Making faces, oh what a delight!
A tapestry woven with quirky threads,
Jumping back from imaginary beds!

With silly wigs and hats askew,
We strike poses like a feline crew.
Tickles exchanged, reflections dance,
In our funhouse, we take a chance!

Colors swirl in laughter's embrace,
While we transform, just a friendly race.
Who needs mirrors when we're this bold?
Our laughter, the treasure, turns to gold!

So grab a brush, let's paint the day,
With joy and humor, come what may.
In this tapestry, we truly shine,
Creating memories, your hand in mine!

Sunsets Beneath Our Stars

Beneath the sun's last playful kiss,
We chase shadows, a silly bliss.
With ice cream spilling, drips and drops,
We giggle loudly, and off it hops!

As skies fade from orange to purple hue,
We spin around, just me and you.
Like dandelions in a cheeky breeze,
Our laughter carried with such sweet ease.

Stars peek out, a sparkly crowd,
Whispers of fun, we laugh out loud.
With each twinkle, we take a chance,
Under the moon, we break into dance!

So let the night cradle our dreams,
In the magic of laughter, nothing's as it seems.
Hand in hand, we wander afar,
In our sunset glow, you are my star!

Starlit Dreams of Unity

Under the moon, we dance and twirl,
With socks that clash in a wild swirl.
Our laughter echoes, a joyful spree,
As we trip on air, just you and me.

Stars wink down with a cheeky glint,
While we argue over who bought the mint.
Moments caught in a quirky frame,
A wobbly duet, but that's our game.

In starlight's glow, we're goofballs grand,
Inventing languages—who can understand?
With pizza slices that fall from the sky,
We feast on dreams and let out a sigh.

Side by side in this jumbled ride,
Even with a hiccup, we take it in stride.
A comedy sketch of cosmic delight,
In our goofy universe, we shine so bright.

Infinite Ties

In a world spun from tangled thread,
We tie silly knots, where others dread.
Chasing after pigeons, we trip and fall,
With a wink and a grin, we stand tall.

Your umbrella's flipped; it flies like a kite,
As rain turns our picnic into a plight.
But we laugh so hard, it starts to rain cheer,
Even puddles join in—there's nothing to fear!

With mismatched socks and cups half full,
We paint each day with splashes of wool.
In the infinite web of our bizarre dance,
We stumble and laugh, and that's our chance.

Together we twirl, our hearts all aglow,
In this wacky tale, we steal every show.
With a wink and a nudge, we make it just right,
In our tangled world, you're my favorite sight.

Kaleidoscope of Togetherness

In a kaleidoscope, we find our view,
With laughter that bursts like bright confetti too.
Your silly hats make the best of fashion,
A runway of giggles, a hilarious passion.

A cup of jellybeans held tight in hand,
While we dance with shadows across the land.
Colors collide in our playful spree,
As time bends back when you laugh with me.

Through a prism of joy, we spin and glide,
In a chorus of chuckles, we tag along for the ride.
Your quirky remarks spark sunshine anew,
In this merry-go-round, it's just us two.

In the great big frame of our dazzling art,
We weave every moment, a colorful start.
Together forever in this silly parade,
In the kaleidoscope, no joy will fade.

Harmonies in the Silence

In the quiet hum, our laughter shakes,
With whispered secrets and silly mistakes.
A muffin falls! Oh, what a delight,
As we giggle softly in the soft moonlight.

We share tales of socks that have gone astray,
While the cat plots a leap in a comedic array.
Chasing shadows under starlit skies,
We compose a symphony of giggles and sighs.

With spoonfuls of ice cream, we orchestrate bliss,
In a harmony forged from every sweet kiss.
Even silence sings when it's wrapped in our quirks,
A melody joyful, no need for the perks.

So here's to the silence that echoes our name,
In this light-hearted dance, we play our game.
With silly serenades in the twilight's embrace,
We find the true magic in our special place.